You Are Not Alone

Poems by
Shauna Darling Robertson

troika

Published by TROIKA

First Published 2023

Troika Books Ltd
Well House, Green Lane, Ardleigh CO7 7PD
www.troikabooks.com

A CIP catalogue record for this book
is available from the British Library

ISBN 978-1-912745-17-3

1 3 5 7 9 10 8 6 4 2

Printed in Poland by Totem.com.pl

Supported using public funding by
**ARTS COUNCIL
ENGLAND**

Also by Shauna Darling Robertson

SATURDAYS AT THE IMAGINARIUM

A National Poetry Day Selection 2021

'A feast of wonder, imagination, possibility, defiance,
strength and awe... to be read, gifted, shared and loved.'
– Bookwagon

'The sort of children's poetry book that should be on the
shelves of all good bookshops. Read these poems to
children, they can't fail to light a spark.'
– Brian Moses

'A beautiful balancing act of the surreal and the graspable...
But always there's a light in the window to guide you to a
home you never imagined before.'
– A.F. Harrold

Contents

The Crate of Air That Will Change Everything   80

Sometimes Like

A Wild Horse

And

Sometimes Like

Disco Lights

What the Mind Is Like

after Miroslav Holub

Officially the mind
is brain-shaped, head-dwelling
and brims with logic

but anyone who's done time with the mind
knows that it's also

vast like the night sky,
terrorising like a carnivore with an automatic weapon
and a quiet ally, like the janitor who gets the job done.

It pulses and purrs like a heart crossed with a kitten
then it's a cloud, a butterfly, a bulldozer.

Sometimes it's like a frightened robot
slamming rusty feet on brakes and 3D-printing concrete walls.

And sometimes like a wild horse.
And sometimes like disco lights.

In it there are keys and sponges,
dust and weather systems

and in it is something you thought you'd lost,
some unwanted things you were given
and something you long for so badly
but don't yet know is already yours.

How Have You Been Feeling Lately?

Over the past month I've had little interest in
frills / holdalls / giving figs

I would describe my mood as
mare-shaped / blowfish / pope-less

Some days I have trouble getting out of
lead / cowhide / birthdays

I've noticed a change in my
engine / appliances / hairspray

More than twice this week I've been
buzzing / muzzled / slumpish

I find it hard to concentrate on
the height of the sun / the 3rd of the month /
the where of the chair

Sometimes I can't help thinking about
hanging spoons on your ears / biting Joan's shoulder /
hiding between my own fingers

Lately my future seems
horizontal / horsewhipped / a horoscope

But between you and me, what troubles me most is
the trouble / between me / and me

I Want to Experience Life in Neutral With No Sudden Movements

I think I hear a dove. It's a thin sound
as if something is going to happen. Bad feelings come
in shades of green. Time is as hard to grasp
as a country I've never been to and when I'm not moving
it feels like my insides and my outsides are trying to swap places.

Good feelings come in pretty colours and feel soft
like cashmere. I like saying the word *optimistic*.
I see the days of the week as going uphill and downhill
and the months are like stairs. *Shocked* is a quick, brutal word.
Things I can't predict or control confuse me.

Dark blue is my anchor. Once I had to keep walking,
on and on. Turning back was not an option because
roads don't come to an end. Sometimes I feel the most alone
when there are people in the room. Numbers are fixed,
unchanging things. When I make a mistake I want to disappear.

I like to have everything where I can see it. My memory is like
a pool of dots. I don't always know what my legs are up to
and I fear if I'm touched all my thoughts will become visible.
When my mind moves too fast for language I jumble up words.
Sometimes it feels like the ground is shaking, the landscape

coming to get me. When a hotel looks different from the website,
I don't know which version to believe. I take everything
literally. When people talk for too long it's like a tsunami
which I cancel out by thinking of music or trains. I can't name
my feelings, don't recognise them. Surprises hurt, almost

physically. I work out that 'defects in social-emotional reciprocity'
refers to how conversations happen. One day I saw myself
in a full-length mirror and realised I was waving goodbye.
My brain is differently wired. I feel assaulted by bright lights.
I set all my clocks ten minutes ahead, it reduces the pressure.

*Note: This is a 'found poem' made up of words and phrases
borrowed from a selection of sources. The sources are listed in
'Notes on Poems' on page 120.*

Ominous Sky

after Chūya Nakahara

one morning   I saw   a black cloud
hanging   up there   in the sky
    the cloud hovered   back and forth   and then
it stole   like a ghost   into my mind

what   made it do that?   why?
did I dream   of rain   of rain
    for so long   that rain came   and made itself mine

was it   the time bomb   of DNA
finally going off   that day   the alarm call
    (ring-ring)   of the pre-arranged   hour of explosion

perhaps a sliver   of some old bruise   that broke off
travelled north   its moisture vaporising   as it rose
        and then   it fell   condensed again

or   did the black cloud look   for shelter
from all the hot air   and mistake my mind   for
    a safe place   or was it   after a soul mate
saw another creature   made almost entirely   of lost tides

Avoidance Is a Common Behaviour When Anxiety Strikes

For fear of hair shame, I wear a hat.
For fear of silences, I'm loathe to chat.
For fear of ups and downs, I take the flat.

For fear of thoughtlessness, I over-think.
For fear of timelessness, I stay in-synch.
For fear of drowning, I hardly drink.

For fear of atmospheres, I never fly.
For fear of modest moods, I chase the high.
For fear of wanting, I buy-buy-buy.

For fear of peace and ease, I start a war.
For fear of order, I break the law.
For fear of not enough, I push for more.

For fear of prominence, I'm rarely seen.
For fear of blemishes, I'm squeaky clean.
For fear of nightmares, I never dream.

For fear of standing up, I tend to crawl.
For fear of free will, I hit the wall.
For fear of fear itself, my life is small.

Sam Asks Alexa About Wellbeing

after George Szirtes

What is wellbeing, asks Sam. It starts with freedom, says Alexa, which spins around until it feels dizzy and then has a little lie down.

What is wellbeing, asks Sam. A giant slice of cake that's reassuringly solid and as light and fluffy as air, says Alexa.

What is wellbeing, asks Sam. A cross between a pillow, a pair of skis and a lioness, says Alexa.

What is wellbeing, asks Sam. A house that can fly, says Alexa.

What is wellbeing, asks Sam. I'm not sure but I think it might be a deep green, says Alexa.

What is wellbeing, asks Sam. A kind of hologram, says Alexa. Imagine looking into the cells of an orange and seeing the whole orange and also every other fruit in there.

What is wellbeing, asks Sam. A rocking chair that's also a rope ladder to the stars, says Alexa.

What is wellbeing, asks Sam. Pages of a book talking and laughing about the times they had when they were trees, says Alexa.

What is wellbeing, asks Sam. The heart and the mind and the world on the same page, says Alexa, or thereabouts.

How to Grow Your Pain

Start a war against it. Fight it.
Shut the door on it, deny it.
Judge, dissect and analyse it.
Anything but feel it.

Swallow it with cheesecake. Feed it.
Drink it, sink it puke and bleed it.
Protein shake and matcha tea it.
Anything but feel it.

Dig a hole and bury, hide it.
Rage and snarl and sneer, to spite it.
Roll it in tobacco, light it.
Anything but feel it.

Selfie, tag and post and tweet it.
Pout and posture look-at-me it.
Wear it like a badge and be it.
Anything but feel it.

Three Short Verses on Air

1.

An ill wind blew through our family
and cast us in all directions.
Dad spiralled away like a sycamore
to put down roots elsewhere.
Mum dropped like a pine cone
to the forest floor.

2.

Breathe in, breathe out.
Breathe in, breathe out.

The air is always there.
It never says
*Not now, can't you see I'm too busy
for oxygenation.*

Sometimes I test its intentions by holding my breath
and refusing its nourishment.

Fifty seconds
is the most I've managed.

It won't take no for an answer,
the air.

3.

The thing I fear most
is the breeze.

Give me gale, tornado, cyclone, hurricane,
tempest, twister, sirocco, squall.

What really unnerves me
is a gentle breeze.

Jamal Wishes He Could Explain It

You'd understand if there were tigers. Or snakes.
Or gangs or landmines I had to get through
which would warrant the dry mouth. The sweating. The shakes.
There'd be logical dangers with tigers or snakes.
Or with a plague. A crime scene. A military coup.
You'd understand, if there were tigers or snakes.
Instead, so much rage and grief to move through.

I Am Literally Gigantic

Seriously - my lungs, laid out
would cover a hundred square metres
which is about the floor space of your whole house

and my blood vessels, outstretched
would travel 60,000 miles
or two-and-a-half times the circumference of Earth

and in my brain I have a nerve fibre network
whose total length is more than the distance
between Earth and the moon.

You say I keep too tight a rein on myself
but don't these dimensions
scare you a little too?

Janek Taps the Window Twenty Times

I've said something stupid, I know it
or I've fired off a text that seemed mean
and that joke I told, did anyone actually laugh

so I tap the window twenty times,
ten with the left index finger, ten with the right,
then I tap out my song -

'Cause I got this
I'm letting it go-go-go
look, it's all gonna be okay

tap tap tap till I've got this,
till it's all (more or less) okay

but I'm always saying dumb stuff
so it's ten with the left index finger, ten with the right

or sometimes (to mix it up) I'll tap out
which gorilla feels sick?
which wildebeest is ill and needs a pill?
or the first five bars of Beethoven's Fifth
and sometimes random lines from *A Wrinkle in Time*
or every second stop on the Piccadilly Line

my tapping fingers tap the tops of tables, the backs of chairs
the wall, the door, my skull, my thigh

and for sure, my fingers sting
and for sure, my nails are split
and for sure, my ears ring
with the constant sound of tap tap tap

still, I can fill a kettle with one hand
while the other hand taps the sink
and while tapping I can make a sandwich,
write a note, water the plants, feed the cat,
button a shirt, play guitar, catch the 66 bus
as I tap and tap and tap and tap

till I've got this,
till it's all
(more or less)
okay.

CHLOE

This is for you
she says,
it's all of my heart.

She's handing you
a deflated rugby ball.
A squashed satsuma.

She's handing you
a pocket whose contents have leaked
through a ripped seam.

She's handing you
a baby bird that fell from the nest
and is barely breathing.

A lump of red meat and jelly,
a mess of molecules and atoms
that's jerking and twitching, like voltage.

This is for you.

Liam Hears a Lot More Than Voices

Inside my head
    windows closed, the house is noisy.
    A half-crazed alley cat is running around wild
    and a pale bird hides under the table

    inside my head. Something dry is catching fire
    and the authorities are firing a jet of questions –
    ten a second, about everything but the fire

    inside my head. The telephone rings and rings,
    a dog will not stop barking barking barking
    and someone wants to know why it's thundering again

    inside my head. Then an angel throws open a window
    and I breathe – breathe - breathe - the spacious air.
    I breathe into the half-crazed cat. The pale bird. The table

    inside my head. I breathe into the fire and let the fire dance,
    let the questions breathe. I breathe ring-ring. I breathe bark-bark.
    I breathe and let the thunder be the thunder that is
                           inside my head.

If We Have More Words for Good Things, Do We Feel Better?

I heard there's a word in Bantu
for the irresistible urge to shed your clothes
while dancing   *Mbuki-mvuki*

In Dutch you need just one word to say
when I go outside and walk in the wind
I come alive   *Uitwaaien*

Norwegians enjoying
a cold drink outside on a hot day
can sum up that feeling with a word   *Utepils*

In the Philippines, a single word captures
that fizzy feeling you get
when you're talking to someone you fancy   *Kilig*

Germans can relax with a word that says
I feel protected
and safe from harm   *Geborgenheit*

In Hebrew there's a word
for sauntering, carefree
down a particular street in Tel Aviv   *Lehizdangef*

Swedes can name
the gentle, welcoming space
between two embracing arms   *Famn*

In English (go figure)
we have a word for this:
the overwhelming desire to kiss   *Basorexia*

WHAT IF I'M NOT

THE SHAPE

OF THE BOXES

ON OFFER?

A Day in the Life of Your Inner Instagrammer

The sun is shining like a smiley sticker
when your #IGer leaps out of bed,
photographs a black bean breakfast taco
and a strawberry smoothie,
shares skincare tips
and a picture of a kitten in a hat
and heads out into the virtual day.

The airwaves are congested, chock-full of other 'grammers
firing off their #Fitspos #OOTDs
#POTDs and #Regrams,
foraging, copying, depositing and pointing
their merciless little spotlights
on everything, on nothing.

It's Selfie Sunday. Your inner Insta shares a post,
asks if anyone else feels like an ant
fabricating hollow networks of tunnels and chambers
and scavenging with bent antennae
for likes, mentions, hypes.

Someone replies with a video –
a colony of ants clearing a rainforest floor
of nearly every living thing
and for a moment, a bunch of other #IGers stop
and the wow emojis start to stack up...
then they all go back to looking at sticky stuff –
dogs, ice-cream, A-listers looking perfect or else looking like shit.

Your 'grammer tries a joke:
what do you call an ant with no real friends?

<Silence>

So much for social insects, you say to yourself,
still unshowered and in slippers at five.

And If Your Friends Jumped in a Lake, Would You Follow Them?

after Daniil Kharms

Susie Masterson jumped in a lake. Josh Winterson saw what happened and immediately jumped in a lake. Aleesha Anand, having heard the news, jumped in a lake the next day. About a week later, Si Jenkins, who had been away on holiday and whose mother had confiscated his phone, jumped in a lake the minute he got home. Si's ex-girlfriend, Olivia, hummed and hawed over the weekend and then jumped in a lake. Olivia's cousin, Julie, who had been following the whole thing on TikTok for the past month and was desperate to join in but didn't live anywhere near a lake couldn't believe her luck when she was dragged to her aunt and uncle's golden wedding anniversary – in the Lake District. It's a good thing they're all swimmers. I'd hate to see anyone sink.

This Is How I Would Like to Belong

If I were a seedling, my mother would be the earth and my father would be sunlight.

If I were the distance, my sisters would be binoculars and my brothers bullet trains.

If my cousins were a jumble of long words, I'd be a dictionary.

If I were a song, my teachers would be notes and ears and pianos and dancers.

If I were a slice of bread, my community would be full of butter and jam, ham and hummus, mustard and Marmite, cheese and yeast and knives and flour and plates and toasters and appetites and taste buds and croutons and tongues.

If I could go nowhere, my country would make of itself a post office and a kaleidoscope.

If I were a leaf, my heart and mind and soul would be trees.

If the world needed sleep, first I'd be the dusk and then I'd be the new dawn.

As If I Should Know by Now

It's the question that won't go away. The question that keeps bearing down on me with its in-your-face urgency, its look-at-me intensity. The question that swells and spreads, accelerates and escalates. What do I want to be? What do I plan to do with this life of mine?

I want to be a sweetshop that only opens on Sundays around lunchtime.

I have my own questions. I question the wisdom of trusting someone so young with such a far-reaching decision. I question the point of planning when the planet's burning up.

I want to burst my oily banks, to be the inch or two of air that surrounds my skin.

And what if I'm not the shape of the boxes on offer, from brand ambassador to contemporary dancer? What if the ways I like to ply my skills aren't so easily monetized? What if I wasn't designed for either/or, what if I need to think and jump, disrupt and build, navigate and imagine, if I'm to thrive? What if I love paper, can't hack printers? Love social change, hate politics? Love bees and honey but come out in hives? What if the world of work leaves me uninspired with its hierarchies, synergies and deep dives? What if, when I lie in the grass looking at clouds I can equally see a future in psychiatry and the beauty industry? When I'm 33, will I remember a single thing from a chemistry GCSE or is it just a ticket, a tick-box, a trick to keep me busy?

I want to freestyle my way through the density of your expectations.

Suppose I get it all wrong. What if I choose X or Y and in that choosing, all the As, Bs and Cs become lost to me and then what if I was really an A person all along, or I look over and see all the Bs having way more fun, and those Cs, well they're assholes but at least they're making a ton of money.

I want to find a syringe in the sky and drain all the pus from this world, give all of our wounds some air.

SO THEN THEY SENT ME TO ART THERAPY

Show me the colour of your fury, she said
and pushed a box of chalks across the table.

Eyes blazing, I snatched the box
and emptied the whole idiotic lot
right into her cream-trousered lap.

A pause. Then she leapt up –
clapped her perfect hands, threw back her head
and laughed and laughed.

Brilliant! Vivid! A psychadelic riot! she hooted,
whirling around in chalk-dust circles, her arms outstretched
and eyes blazing like comets.

In that instant I twigged
that she'd probably once sat
exactly where I was sitting

and I felt sorry about the trousers
but also not sorry at all

so I tried really hard to stay true to my filthy mood
but the hooting and the whirling got hold of me too

till there we were, the pair of us
spinning and twisting and whooping and howling,
thinking, *who knew*
these were the colours of our fury.

MACKENZIE

He pinned his hopes
on just one thing

to aim - to shoot - to score - to win

so when he lost
it did him in.

We Have Been Optimized

When did raking around the neighbourhood
building makeshift go-karts
and trailing sticks along the railings
become supervised playdates?

When we crawled through endless legs,
tugged on trousers with sticky hands and chanted
what's this for and can I have a go at that,
how come you packaged us off to preschool?

We jumped in the lake, legged it down Milton Street,
sang jingles on the bus and messed about with icing sugar.
You signed us up for swimming club, running club,
choir and mini Masterchef.

When we dived into dodge ball and hopscotch,
tag, kick-the-can, marbles and jacks
you dragged us to the Sunday Little Leagues.

When did skateboarding up at the rec
or standing chatting outside the chippy
become red flags for delinquency?

When did a paper round become an internship,
a scabby knee turn into a health and safety issue
and when did we start sitting exams
before we'd even learnt to whistle?

Tell me, when did I sign up
to be trained, tailored, primed and styled
and why, if I've been optimized,
do I falter far more than I rise?

SUVI

wears long sleeves in summer
and we all want to know
what she keeps under wraps.

Embarrassing tattoos, Lewis reckons
but I'm not so sure.

In the far corner of the park that day
I guess I say something
that softens her edges, soothes her defences -

she rolls up her sleeves to the elbows, reveals
a scripture of scars
and dares me to read

not words or verses
but scratches, incisions, punctures, nicks,
lesions and sores, boundaries and borders,
ridges, knots, scabs, burrs.

Go on, she says
so I run my fingers - gently, gingerly
along her lines of battle

and (wincing, flinching)
I feel into
her silent screams –   *Please... relief.*
                            Please... peace.

Thou Shalt Be Immaculate

face cream, hand cream, foot cream, eye cream
shaving cream, anti-ageing cream, day cream, night cream
sun cream, spot cream, fat cream, scar cream

white cream, cold cream, scrub cream, peel cream
hair cream, nail cream, repair cream, cleaning cream,
lip cream, filler cream, vitamin cream, lifting cream

tanning cream, toning cream, mask cream, lash cream
caffeine cream, wrinkle cream, slimming cream, miracle cream
firming cream, screening cream, calming cream, sleep cream

acid cream, mango cream, nut cream, butt cream
straight cream, curly cream, cheap cream, easy cream
boost cream, bubble cream, frizz cream, jazz cream

fresh cream, moon cream, yoga cream, glow cream
smile cream, light cream, lava cream, jungle cream
dream cream, pure cream, renew cream, fuel cream

gym cream, job cream, tick-tick-the-box cream
stand cream, sit cream, yes cream, best cream
single cream, double cream, couples cream, clotted cream

rich cream, gloss cream, cat-that-got-the-cream cream
fake cream, sham cream, whipped cream, soured cream
power cream, now cream, happy cream, SCREAM CREAM

The Mind and the Body Are Not Two Separate Things

About a month ago Syed began
to fall apart.

The first thing to go was his left ear
which snapped off in the frozen food aisle of Tesco.

At the checkout when Syed reached for his wallet
both hands detached at the wrists.

That evening while he was slumped in front of the TV
Syed's legs wandered off to his bedroom

and as he watched them go
his shoulders drifted down towards his waist.

That weekend when Syed's sister came to visit
she found a torso, a mouth, a liver and a spleen
on the kitchen floor.

'What the hell, Syed,' she screamed,
'when you said you were falling apart I thought you meant
mentally!'

Landlocked

Hold the shell to your ear dear, she says
so I take it from her outstretched hand

but drop it back on the sand
since I already know the sound of the sea

it's been moving within me since the day I began -
we were born as one, the sea and me.

Still, somehow I landed
in this family / community / country
of landlubbers

who, with feet firmly planted
sent me to land school
where I earned my place
at the great land academy
to train for a solid future
in land management, land husbandry.

Meanwhile, the tides within me
ebb and flow, rise and fall
and nothing seems to stop them

not even my refusal
of their call.

Hoping to Be Liked

I've thrown a rock then promptly legged it.
Told a story, over-egged it
        for effect.
Scanned the menu, ordered squid.
Taken on a nick-name. Hid
        my intellect.

Told a lie, betrayed a promise.
Claimed to have read Dylan Thomas.
        Become vegan.
Said that I was high on grass.
Pierced an eyebrow. Took a class
        in public speaking.

Sold my soul (the lowest bidder).
Begged an ex to reconsider
        ditching me.
Shrugged and sneered *I can't be arsed.*
Snapped, WhatsApped my private parts
        for all to see.

Stolen something for a dare.
Acted like I didn't care
        and snogged a stranger.
Taken insults on the chin.
Fibbed about the shape I'm in.
        Courted danger.

Squashed a spider. Skipped dessert.
Laughed at friends when they were hurt.
            Put on a tie.
Called a barmaid something vile.
Faked an accent, forced a smile.
            Refused to cry.

I'M JUGGLING A HUNDRED FULL STOPS

I can't stop thinking that the world and everyone in it is a proofreader and I was born with bad grammar and no sense of syntax.

I look in the mirror and all I see is a chin covered with misplaced apostrophes. I never leave the house without a scarf to hide my unsightly speech marks. I walk into a room and freeze: when is it not 'i' before 'e'?

I have a terrible run-on sentences habit which I try to paste over with fake laughter, heavy make-up and comma splices. Sometimes I try to appear superior by wearing heels and gorging on semi-colons; then I feel guilty and silly and end up seeking sympathy by crying over hyphens.

Some days I feel like I'm juggling a hundred full stops and if I drop one, I'll never be able to draw breath again. Each time I open my mouth I see exclamation marks and imagine them all cracking jokes behind my back.

The other day I heard someone refer to me as square brackets and I felt like my life was over. But if I'm honest, I only feel comfortable between parentheses and at the same time I know they're trapping me in a prison of my own making.

Sometimes I just want to march outside, all clauses blazing, and scream, *Seriously? How do you expect me to build coherent sentences in a world where all the textbooks say adverbs are a bad idea while out in the street, people are singing deafeningly, speaking confidently and declaiming convincingly that ellipses are the root of all unfinished business...*

Before Anything Else He Loves Gets Away

He shuts the front door, followed by the back.
Next, he closes all the windows.

He locks up the *namaskārs* and *shukriyas*,
the hellos and thank yous he understands
in a handful of languages.
Then he slams shut the smell of hot summer dust
and several shades of sky blue and mountain green.

It's not long before he closes a whole bunch of books
followed by some songs, the name of his team,
the taste of his mother's fried chicken wings
and the last thing his father told him.

He closes hip-hop, hard rock, R&B.
Sundays at the lake, cricket in the street
and cycling home at dusk past the barley fields.

He zips shut his khaki canvas backpack
and locks down his hips so as not to feel
the insufferable itching in his feet.

He closes his ears followed by his mouth.
He folds his arms, lungs, eyes, his mind.

He shuts his roads, bridges, railways, runways
till every path to his heart seems all but gone

and still the heart keeps beating time
and life (and love, and loss) go on.

Angus Is a No-Show

I dread the shadows looming up ahead
and seek escape by sinking into sleep.
Immobilise myself. Lie down. Play dead
and block emotion. Plug the urge to weep.

I seek escape by sinking into sleep
and hide in the familiar. Crouch. Lay low.
I block emotion, plug the urge to weep.
An invitation? *Maybe.* Never show,

just hide in the familiar. Crouch. Lay low
and quit before I've started. Curl up small.
Invitations? *Maybe.* Then don't show,
just sit around and cower, shrink and crawl.

I quit before I've started, curl up small.
Resist constructive habits to the hilt.
I sit around and cower. Shrink and crawl,
with all self-kindness nullified by guilt.

Resisting helpful habits to the hilt
I snub compassion, push my friends away.
With all self-kindness overturned by guilt
I fade to ever darker shades of grey.

I shun compassion. Keep my friends at bay.
Immobilise myself. Lie down. Play dead,
a hostage of the endless shades of grey.
I dread the shadows looming up ahead.

Wherever I Went, There I Was

so I tried to shrink myself in fad diets
　　　　but ketoed out

so I covered myself in athleisure fashion
　　　　but was so last season

so I buried myself in sci-fi books
　　　　but got stuck on the shelf

so I threw myself into soccer
　　　　but scored an own goal

so I submerged myself online
　　　　but got flagged up as spam

so I purged myself in confession
　　　　but no-one wanted to hear

so I lost myself in you
　　　　and finally, I disappeared.

For this,
　　　　I may never forgive you.

After Mum Died, Dad Made Some Questionable Choices

1. Belinda

I was still small
and she had the mouth of a giant.
A giant that barked *Butterfingers!*

The giant hurled a ball my way
and while I was winded, christened me
                                Butterfingers!

The giant handed me a sandwich,
it landed in the grass to the ring of
                                Butterfingers!

The giant held open the door -
the door that slammed in my face, must've been
                                Butterfingers!

Dad closed the door on Belinda.
Sorry kid, he said. I dropped the ball.

2. Mona

She emerged out of nowhere
with a roll-call of conditions.
Don't, she said.

Don't eat with your hands *don't* put sugar on that *don't* shrug
your shoulders *don't* catch measles *don't* touch my hand *don't*
speak when I'm watching TV *don't* just sit there *don't* fiddle with
your hair *don't* disturb your father *don't* kick that ball against
that wall *don't* ask questions

then one day she went
almost as quickly as she'd come, but

my lungs were choked with *don't*
my guts knotted up with *don't*
my blood ran *don't*, my eyes saw *don't*
my mouth was a monstrous metronome
ticking to the rhythm of *don't*.

Sorry kid, Dad said. *I -*
Don't, I snapped. Just *don't*.

Kyle Said They Thought That Feelings Were Like

rip tides, abducting them from the beach
and biting down to the bone like piranhas.

Thugs and muggers, hunting in packs and multi-tasking -
this one kicks while the other one punches.

Mosquitoes with that drive-you-nuts buzz
then the sting of a piercing, the draining of blood.

The judge, the jury and the heavy sentence
dealt out with one big bang of a hammer.

Really? said Alex.
For me they're like

waltzing to breakbeats.
Atmospheric gases.
Days of the week.

Balancing on clouds.
Little telegrams from shifting landscapes.
The way wheat fields swish in the wind.

Like juice that squirts from an orange
or snowflakes on your tongue
and the minute they land, they're almost gone.

THE WHOLE WORLD IS HERE FOR ME

People are knotty, complex, confusing
so I'm stretching my sense of kin
to include the elements.

Look, I'm pretty sure there are no mean trees
and I've seen the way the grass waves as I pass.

Sometimes the river rises up and asks
if I need something moved, something carried.

The leaves whisper what's happening.
The wind has my back.

I plug myself into the sun and shine.
Yesterday a worm surfaced just to check I was okay

and as I walked away
the stones massaged my soles.

The whole world is here for me
so you people can come, you can go.
You can be as perplexing as you please.

I Asked

The Edge

The Edge

Said Yes

A Little Something Ryan Thought You Should Know

There are certain types of creatures -
some jellyfish, for instance

that light up when they're touched
bright as fibre optics
like you'd flicked some massive on-switch.

I'm not one of those creatures.
Reach out and I flinch.
Touch me and I sting.

Float around, though
(not too close)

give me space to bob about
in my own little waves

and there's a chance my light
might quietly rise.

Occasionally I'll bite
but when I do, please know
I won't have meant to.

Dissociation Is a Mental Process of Disconnecting From One's Thoughts, Feelings, Memories or Surroundings

The first time I saw sadness was from the air.
            I haven't been myself for a long time.
Feeling detached from my body
            in the space of an evening
I display no emotion, opinion or reaction
            it feels as though it never happened
holding a conversation
            has caused whole chunks of my life to disappear.

I know I went to high school
            as if I was seeing the world in a dream.
I'm a person trying my best to play 'me'
            when I'm confused and my feet are cold.
If my body is present, people tend to expect
            the rest of me to be too.
Is anyone ever completely in the room?
            We all end up in places and
            don't know how we got there.

You're Never Too Old for an Imaginary Friend

The panther follows me the full length of the high street
to the bus stop.

The panther sits beside me
on the bus. He has no ticket
and seems to know instinctively
where we're all headed.

He's a big panther,
well-dressed. His shiny black coat is immaculate.
His eyes are supernova yellow.
When they lock onto mine
it's like being set on fire.

Is he kindling a blaze inside me,
lighting all my lamps from within?
Or am I being seared, scorched, marked and charred?

I shrug and ask the panther, *What will you do
when we drive past the zoo?*

He looks at me the way only panthers do,
half hunter, half kitten
and it dawns on me –
this is how it feels to be fully alive.

An Easy Mistake

She sunk her spoon
into a second tub of chocolate spread,
mistaking it for comfort.

He was quick to use his fists
and mistook the distance we kept
for respect.

She drank in the catcalls, the whistles,
intent on mistaking them
for genuine interest.

He grabbed the bottle, the bong
and took swig after hit,
mistaking them for safe spaces.

I pitched my voice in
with the posse of bitching,
which I mistook for belonging.

Come on, don't look at us like that.
If no-one showed you a heart
wouldn't you be easily fooled
by any old piece of meat?

Infobesity

poem ending with a line from a song

infobesity: synonym of information overload ('the availability or supply of too much information, or a state of stress which results from it'); other synonyms: infoglut, infoxication - wiktionary.org

This a.m. I ate
90 newspapers' worth of information
*(there are caves I want to escape to,
drains I crave being rinsed down)*

by midday, I'd put away
10 gigabytes of data
*(sometimes I imagine myself empty inside,
a skinful of vast, white desert)*

after lunch, I chewed through
15 gig of audio-visual images
*(I see deep holes I want to creep into
and pull a duvet the size of Antarctica over me)*

I spewed my name, my gender,
my whereabouts and interests
to 88,000 third parties worldwide

(I long to lie down
and give myself to the anonymous floor)

between the hours of five and ten, I cooked up
20 of today's 300 billion emails

(every word, phrase, subject line I see
reads like a never-ending menu of imperatives)

and in the past 15 minutes
I've dispatched a dozen of 240 million texts
scarfed six of 60,000 GIFs
feasted on 50 of 5 million tweets

(and all the shine of a thousand spotlights,
all the stars we steal from the night sky
will never be enough, never be enough)

Write about a Feeling Without Naming It by Using a Variety of Sentences That Exhibit Your Chosen Feeling in Abstract Terms

This morning I woke up and the ground was still exactly where I left it.

If my thoughts were footwear they would be leather hiking boots, once tight and stiff, now softened with wear, warmth and sweat.

I used to worry about all the crime dramas on TV but now I simply decide: watch them or don't.

When I sing, it's like... who cares what it's like, I just sing!

Yesterday I tried taking everything really personally. It hurt a lot but I didn't die. Isn't that interesting?

Imagine living in a house full of thistles in a village called Prickledown in County Thorn, then along comes a lambswool bus and you get on it and go.

If I had a box of fireworks and a rollercoaster, maybe I could make light and excitement wherever I went from now on. Otherwise, I could try it with something else, like a torch and a spare tyre.

Come dusk, I'll take a walk up Innox Hill so I can look back across town and see all the roofs relaxing.

It Matters Who You Ask

I asked the high

the high said yes

I asked July

July said yes

I asked a deep breath

the deep breath said yes

I asked blood red

blood red said yes

I asked the edge

the edge said yes

I asked a rough sketch

the rough sketch said yes

I asked the laws of motion

the laws of motion said yes

I asked the last hope

the last hope said yes

I asked the speed of light

the speed of light said yes

I asked late at night

late at night said yes

finally, I asked you

and you said no

I crumpled

then I counted
ten yesses
and so...

'Myth #1: Mental Illness Only Affects Certain Types of People'

The thin-skinned. The Finnish and drinkers of tea.
Skinny men. Redheads. Young mothers of three.

Maths teachers. Athletes. Some Mandarin speakers.
Graduates. Zookeepers. Job- and thrill-seekers.

Singles. And marrieds. Suzannas and Spencers.
Dinner guests. Dentists and members of MENSA.

Cat owners. Cry-baby kids. Centre forwards.
Shy people. Tomboys and chairs of the board.

Bass players, rule breakers. Boys yet to shave.
Hecklers. Those who start Mexican waves.

Bartenders, market vendors, over-spenders,
email senders, Facebook frienders, first offenders,
great pretenders, East/West-enders, warm and tenders.

Risk takers, cake bakers, status fakers, holidaymakers.
Ice-skaters, heartbreakers.
Procrastinators. Movers, shakers.

Breakfast skippers, skinny dippers.
Baby sitters, carpet fitters.
Snitchers, bitches, baseball pitchers.

Sergeant-majors, minimum wagers.
Theatre goers, tantrum throwers.
eBay buyers, low/high flyers,
bikers, hikers, hunger strikers.

Jugglers, smugglers, love-to-snugglers.
Wheelchair users, door-key losers.
Dental flossers, total tossers.
Bin men, violinists, builders.
Olives, Emmas, Chitras, Hildas.

Vinyl spinners, lotto winners.
Bloggers, early morning joggers.

Kidnappers, rappers and afternoon nappers.
Pallbearers, swearers and contact lens wearers.
Rihanna fans. Caravanners. People with plans.

Saints. Complainers.
Famous painters.
The hairy chested.
The thermal vested.

Leeds supporters. Teenage daughters.
Stamp collectors, school inspectors.
Metrosexuals, intellectuals.
Newsreaders, cheerleaders.

Backstrokers, chain smokers.
Stockbrokers. Practical jokers.
The often quoted. The newly promoted.

Vegetarians. Libertarians.
Geeks, control freaks. Ancient Greeks.

Visitors to Mississippi.
Inner city kids and hippies.

Home-lovers, nomads.
Heirs to thrones.

Point is,
you are not alone.

Take a Memory You're Struggling to Accept

And hold your memory, as you might hold
an injured bird in your hand

Notice your memory, the way you might notice
a streak of neon in an otherwise ordinary sunset

Breathe in your memory, like you'd breathe in
the damp, salty air at the beach

Sit with your memory, as you might sit
with someone whose house was just broken into

Carry your memory, the way you'd carry
a large package marked 'fragile'

Sip at your memory, like you'd sip
at hot tea on a cardboard-grey day

Make room for your memory, as you might make room
for a guest who has come a very long way

The Chronic Recruitment of the Autonomic Nervous System

I'm thinking of the T in PTSD
and how they used to say it only came
volcano sized, war-torn,
barrelling in like a plague
with the force of a head-on collision.

Now they've cottoned on
to the kind that comes in little daily drips,
in constant trickles, under-the-radar ripples

and how it can parade around in full daylight
or sit (quite nicely) on the furniture at home
disguised as something trusted, something known
that no-one would think to call a terrorist

while the terrors are taking hold inside
running riots of fright and flight and flinch and freeze,
firing the neural networks with SOS appeals

* flashing * flashing * flashing * like paparazzi
zapping their electric shocks and lightning strikes
wailing like all the world's sirens
999.......999.......999

while someone, something
is dialling down (slowly, so slowly)
the line to silent.

Note: PTSD - Post-Traumatic Stress Disorder

Banana Bullies

Bananas idling on street corners and making snide remarks; bananas revving their engines at zebra crossings.

Bananas moisturising, making their skins even more slippery.

Bananas getting jobs in media relations, telling us that yellow is the new black; bananas offering a leg-up to lemons, pomelos and other yellow fruit.

Bananas in a mass pile-on, squashing the juice out of a tangerine that said the wrong thing.

Bananas at the call centre keeping us on hold for weeks, months, years, while they eat crisps and discuss holiday plans.

Bananas buying shares in Amazon and ordering dividends for next day delivery.

Bananas distracting us with reports of a heat wave and/or hurricane so we don't notice them slashing public spending again.

Bananas taking our order for coffee and upselling us energized water and a miniature tin of breath mints.

Bananas being found out, but getting away with it by wearing sunglasses, throwing parties and pointing the finger our way.

What I Wanted

I wanted to meet you here and sit
just you and me, drinking coffee

but a ravenous crow, a rabid chainsaw
a cannibalistic shyness took my tongue

and I couldn't ask. Suppose you said no.
Suppose you laughed. Suppose you spat

and kicked me to the ground and yelled
I'd rather lick sweat! Or, suppose you said yes

and got mowed down, ambushed, murdered
on the way. I wanted to meet you here and sit

just you and me, drinking coffee. But, oh
the risks involved were way, way too great.

Louisa Bailey

Instead of standing
at the waiting room door
burying her face in a clipboard
and barking out my name

she came over, put her hand
on my shoulder.
Ready? she asked
ever so gently.

I swallowed,
nodded
and thought about what Mum used to say
about the kindness of strangers.

Louisa Bailey. Her name
was printed on a white badge.
I remember it sometimes,
on days like today.

Gillian Isn't Difficult

Scene 1

    Urgent message from school -
    Handwriting hopeless STOP. Homework late STOP.
    Disrupts the class STOP. Fidgets nonstop STOP.
    Stares out of window STOP. Attention span near-zero STOP.
    Tests failed STOP. Education wasted STOP.

Scene 2

    Marching orders from mother.
    Best dress on - tick! Shiny shoes - tick! Hair tied - tick!
    We're off to see the wizard...
    'STOP – psychiatrist!'

Scene 3

    Oak panelled office. Big desk.
    Tweed jacket. Big man.
    Big leather couch -
    little feet
    can't reach the floor.

    Mother and man
    talk - look - look - talk.
    Mustn't wriggle.
    (Sit on hands.)

    Man stands up, beckons mother to follow.
    To me: *wait here please.*
    Off they go –
    and he flicks on the radio...

Scene 4

Alone at last and   free   to m o v e

sh ff le   sh.ft   *shimmy* s w i ŋ

rise   leaP   s w o o p   spr i n g

F L Y r r y

(Something I don't know: two faces at the window).

Scene 5

Man turns to mother -

Gillian isn't 'difficult'.
She needs to move to think.
See the natural grace, the elated face,
the total focus, almost a trance.
Problem child? The girl's a born dancer!

End credits

On the advice of the psychiatrist, Gillian's mother took her daughter to dance school. Gillian Lynne went on to attend London's Royal Ballet School and to join the Royal Ballet Company. Later, she formed her own musical theatre company and became one of the most accomplished choreographers of our time. With Andrew Lloyd Webber, she created the hugely successful musical theatre productions *Cats* and *The Phantom of the Opera*.

Cassandra

She fashioned a functional family
from pipe cleaners, clothes pegs
and crepe paper.

When they failed to show their faces for a week,
she racked her brain for reasons.

Maybe someone put lemonade in their petrol tank?
Perhaps they accidentally ate their own shoes for breakfast?

What if, on their way home, they were assailed
by a gang of vampire bats, or kidnapped by giant bees?

Clearly, it had to be something extraordinary.
Highly irregular, said Cassandra. *Most unlike them.*

More like her other family,
the one made of skin and bone
and blood that pulsed with unpredictability.

Buffalo This, Buffalo That

Athletics or art. Ocean or desert.
Kitten or buffalo – no matter what,
if there's something you love
then figure it in.

Forget the folks who claim
life's not all buffalo this, buffalo that.
Point at the antelope-shaped horizon and say
See that? Perfect spot for a buffalo
as you figure out
how to figure it in.

One day, a boy will be walking down Main Street
and he'll see a buffalo parked on a double yellow.
In the bistro, a woman will order a Greek salad with fries
and they'll be brought to her by a buffalo.
At night, as the scientist lies sleeping,
the buffalo will come to him in a dream.
A girl will fire up her buffalo
and ride off towards her destiny.
When the police hammer down the door,
the man they're after will be long gone
and all they'll find will be a few buffalo hairs.

Buffalo everywhere.
You figured it in.

How to Rock at Self-Care

Hot soaks and scented candles
aren't for everyone. Frankly I'd flip
if I found bits of dried wildflower in my bathwater
and if you ask me to sit and meditate at sunrise
I'll probably tell you where to stick your little Zen bell.

But stick on some ambient tunes, give me some dancing room
and I'll out-trance anyone.

Sometimes I make a list
of all the stuff that's bugging me
and I rip it up into little bits, fling them into the air
and whirl like a dervish
as the bits and bugs rain down around me.

My sister sings
all the way down Middleton Street,
getting louder up towards the fields
and by the time she reaches Westbury Hill
she's belted out a high C for a good sixteen beats.

Jamie swears by shouting at the wind
and reckons making a six-layer sandwich works too.
Or taking a nap.
Or sprinting barefoot on the beach at low tide.

Sometimes I say a word that's worrying me
over and over till it's just a sound in my mouth.
Other times I imagine I'm the whole room.
Or the universe. Or a speedboat. Or a bear.

Like I said, hot soaks and scented candles aren't for everyone.
Respect the 'self' in self-care.

THE CRATE OF

AIR

THAT WILL

CHANGE

EVERYTHING

In That Year Our Language Changed Along With Our Lives

(for 2020)

happy birthday to you   outbreak
   elbow bump   unknown cause
      herd immunity   surge

  happy birthday   national emergency
basic necessities   suspended   cancelled
   non-essential retail   unprecedented
      for essential medical reasons

happy birthday   no easy options
   lockdown   lockdown   lockdown   lockdown
     how to wash your hands   stay at home
       one form of exercise   save lives
   panic buying   reasonable excuses

  happy birthday   loss of taste or smell
 hands-face-space   halt the spread
      flatten the curve   #ClapForOurCarers
daily death toll   brain fog   Blursday
    homeschool   the Miley Cyrus
  indoors trousers   furloughed

happy birthday   quarantine
overzoomed   support bubbles   coronababies
        keep calm and carry on   doomscrolling
self-isolated   sanitised   coroanacuts
        anti-maskers   vaxxers   covidiots
moronas   the coronalusional
    socially distanced   superspreaders
asymptomatic   air bridges
        staycation   track & trace   pingdemic
coronadodging   circuit-breaker

happy birthday   a new or continuous cough
        first wave   second wave   third wave
            the roadmap   jab, jab, jab
    world-beating   scariants
the new normal
        happy birthday to you

I Realise That There Are Some Serious Holes in My Curriculum

We've done estimation, algebraic manipulation
and function notation. We've learnt angles,
vulgar fractions. Variation. Indices, matrices,
graphical representation of inequalities.

We're doing Rosemary Dobson and *The Three Fates*,
Seamus Heaney's *Mid-Term Break*,
Sonnet 29 by Edna St Vincent Millay
and Lucy, dwelling *Among the Untrodden Ways*.

We've tackled 1848, the revolutions they call 'Springtime'
and how international peace collapsed by 1939,
discussed disagreements in the Treaty of Versailles
and how and why nineteenth-century Italy was unified.

We're scanning Newton's laws of motion and the origins
of our oceans, honing in on homeostasis and the basics
of cellular respiration, debating the concept of a nation state
and the rise of urbanisation, exploring ecosystems,
endothermic reactions, volcanic faults and fractures,
counting causes and costs of the top five greenhouse gases.

Academically I'm winning - top.
Personally I'm spinning - lost.

What I'd most like to be taught?
How to live with this turmoil of thoughts.

THINGS TO THINK

after Robert Bly

Think in ways
you're not used to.
Think in ways
no-one taught you to think.

When the dentist instructs you
to open wide,
think of it as an invitation
to get to know yourself better.

Think of the daily news
as a giant remote control
in need of new batteries.

Think of every call centre
as a room full of poets
getting paid to quote you five sublime lines.

Think that the sky is alive
with an atmospheric presence
that smells of warm bread, cut grass and coffee
and wants what you want, wants what we all want

and when the doorbell rings
think that the delivery guy is bringing
the crate of air that will change everything.

SINCE THEY DID AWAY WITH SUNDAYS

I'm helping myself to...

a dive under the duvet day... a two feet
on the brake day... a hold reality at bay day...

an old jumper and yesterday's socks day... an all rock
and no clock day... a canned soup and popcorn day...

a hands off the wheel day... a hide my light
from the sky day... a go easy on the breeze day...

a picking at the heart's blisters day... a kick a ball
at a wall day... a thinner than water day...

a dangling with monkeys day... a dogs and
midday shade day... an ironing the moon and stars day...

a ploughing the air day... a shower
of violins day... a waiting in for flowers day...

an all off the chest day... a disconnect
the call day... a not-at this-address day...

a gratis day... a brake...
a day of rest...

No

Just for today, I will not stand up straight.
I will not speak when I'm spoken to.
I won't be up by eight or back by ten.

I will not share. I won't pipe down, step up,
pitch in, chill out, eat a decent lunch
or say something constructive.

I will not look sharp or think smart.
I won't try, strive, achieve or succeed.

I will not close my mouth when I chew.
I won't pull my socks up, won't get a grip,
will not chase an A for effort
and will absolutely not be more like you-know-who.

I won't join in, take part, suck it up or calm down.
I will not get a move on, won't go to my room
or wait till anyone's father gets home.

I will not
stop being so ridiculous.

Just for today, I will not aim to please.
So the ball's in your court -
will you please let me be?

Other Side Effects Include

1. You are daily plagued by an urgent desire to watch the wind blowing leaves across a field.

2. Your favourite sandwich tastes like a pocket diary.

3. Each time a song lyric says 'yeah' you see a blue-green glow followed by three quick flashes of Lady Gaga's ankles.

4. Suddenly you own nothing, while anyone who has ever cut your hair becomes inexplicably rich.

5. On the way to the library you invent acceptance speeches using lines from Bugs Bunny. On the way back, you identify more with Bart Simpson, who you now believe to have been the frontman of an ambient house anarcho punk barbershop band.

6. You hear a voice telling you to throw yourself away and while you're wondering which self should do the throwing and which the being thrown, your backpack disappears.

7. Once every couple of weeks you hear the words 'why yellow?', which brings on a sensation of severe imperfection lasting a full three days.

8. When evening comes you go out to the cycle path, lie down on the tarmac and ask gravity to explain itself in its own words.

9. You come to realise that how you feel about any of this is hardly the point since all opinions, spread-eagled, sound like crows calling back and forth.

10. Friends and family are under the impression that you should be universally improved and are gravely disappointed to find that you still experience stress, binge on toast, shop recreationally and are rude to most people.

I Thanked the Sky

You should be bloody grateful,
she'd barked that morning as I stormed out,
her eyes narrowed to a squint, voice shaking with rage.

So, in Group that afternoon
when you suggested the practice of gratitude
as 'an approach to emotional regulation',
an antidote to feelings of hostility, worry, resentment, irritation -
well, it was my turn to get snarky.
Sod that, I spat.

I walked home alone
up past the football field, dragging my feet
while the sun, on its way down, turned my horizon
into a blinder of a lightshow –
scarlet, violet, honey, flame, flamingo
and suddenly I felt it
here, in my chest, like my heart and soul were
alive and on fire
and (without even thinking) I thanked the sky.

When I got home she was out.
Relieved, I thanked the empty house.

I thanked the air
for not being full of arguments.

An hour later, I heard the front door.
Thinking no-one was in
she went straight to the kitchen, sat down
and sobbed.

Mum, I said gently. She startled.
Look, I know it's been hard since...
I just want to say thanks for...
She smiled, cried harder still
and pulled me into a tight, tight hug.

I smiled too, and inside myself
I thanked Group, I thanked you.

Shape Shifter

Never again, I said
and to make damn sure
I stole into the body of a wolf.

I entered by the back door –
a messy business
and shoved my way through gore and guts
past half-digested lambs
and decomposing grandmothers.

My plan was simple: curl up tight,
get under the skin,
let the wolf do all my living,
all my bidding.

But the minute I was in, he took off
like his tail was alight.

His savage shape thundered
across the grey landscape,
blood gunning through his veins,
fluids spewing and gushing

through my nose, in my ears, down my throat
and I gagged and choked,
drowned and spat,
clung and puked
and struggled and scratched

but the wolf paid no mind, just streamed and coursed

then stopped.
Stock still.
In a moonlit spot.

He sniffed the air,
every inch of fur twitching,
heart thumping and pumping

as if the night sky were some kind of
invocation

and as the base of his skull
pinched, tipped back

it was *my* teeth,
my tongue,
my lungs
that gave forth

for the howl
that spoke for us both.

PUMMELLING

I have no scars
to show you. The authorities hold
no record of events.
I was never once hit, bitten or kicked
but –

there were only so many times I could hear
how stupid and useless I was.
How chubby, how glum.
How pig ignorant, oblivious.
How rude and how wrong,
how late, how to blame,
how brass-necked, how brazen,
how hopeless and pointless,

only so many times
before the bruising began.
The yellow, the purple,
the black and the blue
spreading under my skin.

In my bones, in my blood.
In my lungs and my throat.
In my tongue, in my sinews.
My *fuck yous*. My fists.

Holding Out Hope

poem opening with a Chinese proverb

'If I keep a green bough in my heart,
the singing bird will come.'

but what if I keep a black boot in my heaven | a pink
bowl in my heart-throb | a blue boundary in my hedge |
a brown boycott in my heckler | a red brandy in my hemline
| an orange bow-wow in my heliport | a yellow belly
in my helter-skelter | a purple brainstorm in my helmet?

yes, yes and yes –
doesn't matter what, or where

hold out, keep up, hang in there

rule of thumb -
the singing bird
will come.

Let's Make Something of Ourselves

instead of bending out of shape
to fit moulds not of our making.

Something like a sweeping horizon
that's unfarmed, exposed
and says yes to all weathers.

Like adjoining rooms where all the doors
open from whichever side you're on.

Let's stand on each other's shoulders
not in a pyramid of winners and losers
but a towering question mark of curiosity.

Let's mix and discuss, plant seeds that carry within them
all the know-how needed to grow a forest
and pool our resources like a river of collective kindness
so mighty, Amazon will look like a dribble.

Let's make of ourselves something grateful
and humane. Something bold, audacious,
free, warm and safe.
Something that knows it can trust itself
without ever again needing
to be tamed.

Things People Have Told Me in the Past Few Weeks

You need a strong core to excel at rock climbing.
If I go to Edinburgh, I'll have a blast.
We can be short-sighted and long-sighted, both at the same time.
As an actor, Michael Cera has often been typecast.
Most of our communications have moved online.

There are so many things that need to be assessed
when you're choosing a new wheelchair.
In English, there are more than forty ways to say 'yes'.
I really ought to listen to Lily Allen's *Not Fair*.
Young people suffer from higher rates of loneliness.

My new blue shirt looks really great.
In Yiddish, a grumbly person is called a kvetch.
The West has let down Afghanistan in so many ways.
Bolivia's top two languages are Spanish and Quechua.
Most people don't really know what to say.

When people feel seen and heard, given the time of day,
they're far more likely to rise, to shine.
The first writing media were tablets made of clay.
Here's a conversation starter: 'I feel lonely sometimes.
Do you ever feel that way?'

Jasmin's Ladder of Gradual Exposure

Leguminophobia: an irrational fear of baked beans.

10. Look at baked beans on the moon through a telescope.

9. Imagine tiny baked beans no bigger than an ant.

8. Listen to that song where I'm pretty sure the lyrics go, *I'm so sick of this baked bean love.*

7. Laugh at a comedy video involving baked beans.

6. Stop referring to *babies* and start using the words *baked beans.*

5. Walk past the canned vegetables aisle without a blindfold and full riot gear.

4. In the park, stop avoiding the young mother whose toddler's face looks like a baked bean.

3. See baked beans on a menu and don't come back that night and spray-paint the café window black.

2. When skateboarding, stuff baked beans in the knee and elbow pads for added protection.

1. Vote for baked beans in the next things-that-go-great-with-toast election.

A Short History of Mortification

When I opened my mouth
and birds flew out
there was laughter, sneering,
scorn and doubt.
There was shame. Shame. Shame.

When I raised my hand
and ripped open the sky
there was anger, fury,
blame and I
felt the shame. Shame. Shame.

When I swung my hips
and they swung out of tune
there was mockery, mirth
and I wasn't immune
to the shame. Shame. Shame.

With my mouth shut tight and my hand held low,
with my rigid hips
through the world I go -
invisible, timid, compliant and tame.
Such a shame. Shame. Shame.

CHOOSE PLAY

'A Manhattan mother is suing her 4-year-old daughter's preschool, calling it "one big playroom" that deprived the child of the edge needed to get into an elite elementary school.'
Reuters, 2011

Choose running.   Choose jumping.
        Choose dressing up.
                Choose painting.   Choose making.
        Choose messing about with your mates.
    Choose building a den.   Choose rollerskates.

'The creation of something new is not accomplished by the intellect but by the play instinct.' - Carl Jung, psychiatrist and psychoanalyst

Choose cartwheels.   Choose handstands.
        Choose hide and seek.
Choose daisy chain making.   Choose three-legged races.
        Choose climbing a tree.
    Choose sand in your toes.   Choose skimming stones.
Choose daydreaming.   Choose make-believe.

'To truly laugh, you must be able to take your pain, and play with it.' - Charlie Chaplin, comic actor

Choose drumming on upturned buckets with sticks.
Choose muddy puddles.
Choose kicking a ball.   Choose making a swing.
Choose humming.   Choose whistling.
Choose singing at the top of your lungs.
Choose rolling down hills.   Choose skinny dipping.
Choose clowning around.   Choose hanging upside down.

'And forget not that the earth delights to feel your bare feet and the winds long to play with your hair.' - Kahlil Gibran, poet & philosopher

Choose leapfrog.   Choose kicking leaves.
Choose tinkering.
Choose hopping - skipping – bouncing - twirling.
Choose whispering with imaginary friends.
Choose piggy-back rides.   Choose outside.
Choose doodling.   Choose dawdling.
Choose balancing.   Choose wandering.
Choose kite flying, food fights, hopscotch, water bombs.
Choose gazing at the night sky while riding a bike.
Choose making snow angels.   Choose sitting on a wall.
Choose pleasure.   Choose fun.
Choose anything you like.

'Play energizes us and enlivens us. It eases our burdens. It renews our natural sense of optimism and opens us up to new possibilities.' - Stuart Brown, MD, founder of The American National Institute for Play

HAPPINESS

IS

A

HUMMINGBIRD

Because I Broke

after Jenny Joseph

(Down)

The sun was strangled by the sky
because I broke
and the moon suffocated the stars.

The mountains cast shadows across the valleys
because I broke
and the woods hummed with a hollow moan
as the rivers burst their banks
with the grief of the world which
because I broke
was no longer needed.

The shops pulled down their shutters, nailed up signs –
broke.
Way out west all the cowboys dismounted,
the whole game up now because I broke.

(Through)

Today when the sun rises, it means it,
because I broke
and shoots burst up thirsty from the ground.

So what if the waters are still glacial?
Because I broke
I am now my own wetsuit
and possess all the know-how needed to remake myself
as polar bear or seal.
Because I broke
I can dive / drink / float anywhere.

The people in the streets avoid each other's eyes.
I broke
and so I gaze unfazed into all of their souls,
stark naked with compassion because I broke.

I Wanted to Know What Happiness Is So I Googled It

Happiness is 'the feeling of being happy'.
Happiness is looking down on your home town from a plane.
Happiness is consuming a lot of human energy.

Psychologists have come up with a term, *subjective well-being*.
Happiness is a recipe for disappointment.
Happiness is a choice.

Happiness for me is reminiscing about good times with a friend while I indulge in some Nando's chicken, or receiving a standing ovation at the end of a theatre performance.

Happiness is an equation.
Happiness is fake.

The term happiness is used in the context of mental or emotional states, including positive or pleasant emotions ranging from contentment to intense joy.

Happiness is tropical drinks.
Happiness is hard to measure.
Happiness isn't enough.

Happiness is equal to the events of your life minus your expectations of how you want life to be.

Happiness Is Inc. is a brand of casual and athletic clothing made in Canada.
Happiness had to be withdrawn from sale.

You won't become happy merely by socializing with your best friends and achieving your goals. You also need $75,000.

Happiness is a couple of techniques away.
Happiness is good for your health.
Happiness is a hummingbird.

Happiness is intangible, you can't put it in your pocket and save it for later.
The word 'happiness' derives from the term for good fortune, or 'good hap'.
Happiness is like keeping fit, you have to work out.

Happiness is to be found in embracing failure.
Our relentless effort to feel happy is what makes us miserable.

It may be that we're not designed for happiness.
And what is it we were designed for?
'To avoid getting eaten by predators,' says Dr Deaton. 'If nothing eats you today you ought to be happy. At least it's a start.'

Y'ALRIGHT?

'Fine thanks'   Cold, like the blade on an ice-skate.
                 Sunken and lost without trace.
                 Wounded and heartsick and helpless.
                 Vague and stuck. Drained, numb and spaced.

'Not too bad'   Buoyant and daring. Decisive.
                 Vigorous, potent, alive.
                 Eager, dynamic and vibrant.
                 Up, like a walking high five.

'Never better'   Left out, ignored and passed over.
                 Low, like a foot with no shoe.
                 Frantic, as anxious as wasps in a web.
                 Tortured. Torn. Pitiful. Blue.

'Yeah, okay'   Open and chirpy. Responsive.
                 Wrapped in a happy cocoon.
                 Mellow and playful. Uplifted.
                 Balanced. Elated. In tune.

'Peachy'   Furious, brooding and spiteful.
                 Caustic. A full-body scowl.
                 Stewing like toads in a hot tub.
                 Petulant, vengeful and foul.

'M'alright'   Centred and clear as a crystal.
                 Tranquil, serene and at ease.
                 Timeless and free and unbounded.
                 Floating in sunshine and peace.

You Know Cathy, Right?

'Yeah, mouth like a riot!'

'No, lost for words. Quiet. And mild, a bit drippy.'

'Sarcastic, snippy (but sometimes quite kind).'

'She would rob you half blind!'

'Driven. Ambitious. Competitive. Vicious.'

'She's glum and morose.'

'In-your-face, grandiose.'

'Mousey, bookish and smart.'

'A trash-talker, tart - always stoned, drunk, delirious.'

'Diligent. Serious.'   'Rigid. Uptight.'

'Different club every night!'

'Look, she's lazy and feckless.'

'She's spirited, reckless.'

'An ego. Cocksure.'

(Frightened. Lost. Insecure.)

MELISSA, TUESDAY

Then suddenly she smiled
and the week began again.

Where did that smile come from,
did it blow in from the street?

Everything about her
had been sad, tired.
Defeated (almost).

But then,
clouds part.
Ice melts.
Mists rise.

PLEASE TAKE ME BACK TO THE OXFAM SHOP

This family isn't mine. I'm not the same line
        and I felt more at home on the jumbled shelves

                with the battery-less plastic alarm clocks
        and the non-matching wine glasses

                with the battered, bleached-blue paperbacks

and the bric-a-brac of knick-knacks
        with the mis-chosen, missed-the-mark gifts

of empty photo frames and unplayed games
        the still-wrapped puzzles that no-one dared tackle

                the not-so-easy listening CDs
        (somebody/nobody sings the blues)

                the slightly scuffed shoes

the ill-fitting knitwear, shirts that clung too tight
        all going for a song.

        So please take me back
            to the place where I belong, with the others of my kind.
                        This family isn't mine.

Respite

This morning I wished him
gone.

Didn't mean to, I swear -
he's my all, he's my blood
but

the weirdness, the slumps
and the ranting. The dread
of what might happen next.
Then the rages. The fits.

Look, some days I'm just tired,
all this stuff I can't fix

like my life, it's on hold,
it's all *sorry, I can't.*
It's all locked and alarmed

and it isn't his fault
and it isn't his choice

but sometimes (oh god)
just the sound of his voice...

One Whole Minute

So this morning when I was getting ready,
instead of ruminating and cogitating,
I spent one whole minute
feeling the shower's hot rain
pitter-pattering in mini rivers over my shoulders.

When I left the house to get the bus,
instead of cogitating and deliberating,
for one whole minute I listened
to the city rumbling and hissing
and going about its business.

At lunchtime in the canteen,
instead of deliberating and mulling and brooding,
I stood in the queue and for one whole minute, inhaled
till I knew exactly what was on the menu
and what I felt like tasting today.

On the bus back,
instead of mulling and brooding and chewing over,
I sat beside Hayley and for one whole minute
gave her my total, unbroken attention
while she went on and on about Justin again.

Then tonight, while you were all watching TV,
instead of chewing over and ruminating,
I sat for one whole minute and watched each of you, watching
and your eyes, your faces were priceless,
how they moved between tiny frowns and little smiles.

DOWN

They call them *moods*
but suppose they're tsunamis,
mile-high walls of black water
thundering towards the guts, the lungs.

They call them *swings*
but what if they're wild dogs
howling for the moon
while settling for scraps of rank apathy.

They call them *episodes*
but let's say they're hurricanes
ripping up routines, days and hope by the roots
and pummelling the sunrise to rubble.

They call them *bouts*
but to me these are soldiers
marching to the thud of muddled drums
in vice-tight boots under enemy orders.

Still, sometimes
tsunamis subside.
Wild dogs nap.
Hurricanes abate.
Soldiers take leave.

Up

And suddenly I feel like I'm dancing with pandas
and shaking out the lion's mane!

For weeks I've been manifestly *meh*
but now I've kicked off the midday devil
and I'm riding the diamond unicorn with a face full of spring air!

I'm seizing the moon by the teeth
and swallowing strawberry monkeys by the dozen!

I've hooked my atoms to the sun, I'm trading quips
with the Fresh Prince, I'm surfing the waves of Nazaré!

Something's made my roof fly off, I'm all curves and no brakes
and holding a hallelujah licence big enough to cure hiccups!
I'm throwing flowers at myself, I'm swimming in silk,
I'm restringing all the world's instruments!

Yeah, sure, I know it'll pass
but now that this song's been strummed in my guts
I know I have within me the notes I need

to unwrap the package,
to get all rice and peas, to wow the crowd
and feel like the first bite
on all the world's fudge brownies.

Reasons

poem ending with a line by Matt Haig

Because this isn't the end of it, it's the beginning. Because there's music out there that will make you jump till you drop. You'll get chatting to someone over coffee and you'll still be talking to them at lunchtime the next day.

Because you'll make something with your hands and be crazy proud of it. You'll stand under a waterfall and feel its power gunning in your blood. You'll get to choose your own bed and it'll be the most comfortable bed ever.

Because you'll meet a whole new tribe and finally feel like you belong. Because you'll pitch up at the wildest festival on earth and amaze yourself. You'll stick at something, practise it over and over and get your first taste of mastery.

Because you'll discover you can belong in all kinds of different places and faces. Because someone will really need or want something and you'll willingly give it. There are books you'll lose yourself in and books you'll find yourself in.

Because you'll still make rude words in alphabet spaghetti and have fits of giggles over farts. Because you'll discover how, when you like yourself, lots of things seem quite a bit easier. You'll live in a city filled with spaces you'll call home.

Because you'll run until your breath burns in your chest and you'll hike as far as a horizon most people will never see. You'll travel with a toolbox for the bad days and the tools will mostly work. When they don't, there'll be signposts and kindness and an inner grit you'll have learned to count on.

You'll let someone you cherish run their fingers over your skin. You'll open your throat and throw your voice in with other voices to shout and sing about love and justice and power and revolt. One day, in the woods, you'll connect with a crow and feel sure that the pair of you shared a conversation.

You'll be glad you stayed. It won't always be easy but it will be worth it. You'll look back and thank yourself for your courage. *Because you will one day experience joy that matches this pain.*

Tonglen

Breathing in, I swallow your sorrow
which is my sorrow

Breathing in, I drink in your bile
which is my bile

Breathing in, I sip on your smallness
which is my smallness

Breathing in, I gulp down your guile
which is my guile

Breathing in, I guzzle your worries
which are my worries

Breathing out, with all my love
a smile.

Tonglen, or 'giving and taking', is a Buddhist meditative practice. It reverses our usual habit of avoiding suffering and seeking pleasure. In tonglen practice, we visualize taking in others' negativity with every in-breath and sending out whatever will benefit them on the out-breath. The purpose isn't to take on their suffering, but to feel compassion for ourselves and others, and to experience our shared humanity.

Notes on Poems

'What the Mind Is Like' (p 10) is after (which means 'in the style of') Czech poet Miroslav Holub's poem 'What the Heart is Like', published in: Miroslav Holub, *Poems Before and After, Collected English Translations* (Bloodaxe Books, 2006).

'I Want to Experience Life in Neutral with No Sudden Movements' (p 12) is a found poem that collages phrases from five different voices on neurodoversity: *The Reason I Jump: One Boy's Voice from the Silence of Autism* by Naoki Higashida (Sceptre, 2014); *Odd Girl Out: An Autistic Woman in a Neurotypical World* by Laura James (Bluebird, 2017); two close friends of Shauna's (on dyslexia and ADHD) and a conversation overheard in a library (on synaesthesia).

The format of 'Ominous Sky' (p 14) is inspired by Japanese poet Chūya Nakahara's poem 'Overcast Sky', published in the magazine *Modern Poetry in Translation* (No.1, 2020).

'Sam Asks Alexa About Wellbeing' (p 16) is after 'Child Helga and her father' by George Szirtes, examples of which you can find online at http://georgeszirtes.blogspot.com/2013/03/child-helga-and-her-father.html.

'And If Your Friends Jumped in a Lake, Would You Follow Them?' (p32) is inspired by the style of the Russian absurdist poet Daniil Kharms.

The title of 'Before Anything Else He Loves Gets Away' (p48) is taken from a line in Naomi Shihab Nye's poem 'The Lost Parrot', published in her collection *Everything Comes Next: Collected and New Poems* (Greenwillow Books, 2020).

In 'Infobesity' (p62), the final three lines in italics are lyrics from the song 'Never Enough' from *The Greatest Showman* soundtrack written by Benj Pasek and Justin Paul.

The title of 'Write about a Feeling Without Naming It by Using a Variety of Sentences That Exhibit Your Chosen Feeling in Abstract Terms' (p64) was a writing prompt posted by the poet Jack Underwood on Twitter.

'Take A Memory You're Struggling To Accept' (p69) is inspired by an exercise in *A Liberated Mind: The essential guide to ACT* (Acceptance and Commitment Therapy) by Steven C Hayes (Vermillion, 2019).

The mini play-poem 'Gillian Isn't Difficult' (p74) is based on a true story told in chaper one of the book *The Element: How Finding Your Passion Changes Everything* by Sir Ken Robinson and Lou Aronica (Penguin, 2010), available online at www.penguinrandomhouse. ca/books/302886/the-element-by-sir-ken-robinson-phd-with-lou-aronica/9780143116738/excerpt.

'Things To Think' (p85) is after Robert Bly's poem of the same name, published in his book *Morning Poems* (HarperCollins, 1998).

In 'Choose Play' (p100), the news quote about the Manhattan mother suing her 4-year-old daughter's preschool is from Reuters, 2011: www. reuters.com/article/us-lawsuit-preschool-idUSTRE72D7FA20110314.

'Because I Broke' (p104) borrows a form from 'The Sun Has Burst the Sky' from Jenny Joseph's *Selected Poems* (Bloodaxe, 1992). You can also read Jenny's poem online at https://poetryarchive.org/poem/sun-has-burst-sky.

'Reasons' (p116) is inspired by Matt Haig's book *Reasons to Stay Alive* (Canongate, 2015). It is also a true story and features some of the things that Shauna has experienced because of staying alive. The poem ends with a line of Matt's quoted from the book.

Thanks

Shauna would like to offer her heartfelt thanks to everyone who has contributed ideas, thoughts, conversations, resources and editorial suggestions during the writing of this book. So many books, poets, mental health charities, websites, libraries and social media posts have been invaluable as sources of information and inspiration, as well as in-person and online conversations with the members of 'Strange Cargo' and 'The Hours' writers' groups, Louisa Campbell, Stephen Lightbown and Brice Morgan.

Particular thanks are due to Roy Johnson at Troika for mentoring the book throughout, and to Olivia Tuck, whose incisive editorial input has made a world of difference.

Thank you to Wendy Mach for collaborating so creatively and patiently on the book's layout, design and cover artwork.

Shauna is grateful to have received support from Arts Council England's 'Developing Your Creative Practice' programme to support work on *You Are Not Alone*.

About the Author

Shauna Darling Robertson grew up in the north-east of England and currently lives in the south-west. Her poems for adults and children are widely published in anthologies and have been performed by actors, displayed on buses, used as song lyrics, made into short films and turned into comic art. Shauna's first collection for young people, *Saturdays at the Imaginarium* (Troika, 2020), was a National Poetry Day 2021 selection.

Shauna has personal experience of anxiety and depression.

www.shaunadarlingrobertson.com

P.S. Ottava Rima for a Hard Winter

I wrote these lines during a recent difficult period, to remind myself that I'd been through dark times before and got through them. I'm tucking them in at the end here, in case there comes a day when you might need reminding of your own resilience too.

When all around you seems to fall away
and, short of breath, the chilled air snaps and bites,

when what was once alive sinks in decay
and shadows loom in places that were bright,

when joy and hope and spirits fade to grey
and spring and summer colours shrink from sight,

when daytime brings no let-up from the dark,
remember, love: within you burns a spark.

'If you have the words, there's always a chance
that you'll find the way.'

Seamus Heaney

The home of great children's books

Troika is a small independent children's

book publisher. We're based in the UK.

www.troikabooks.com

Follow us on social media

  @TroikaBooks

  @troikabooks